There never was a finer day

And never will be while May is May

JAMES LYNCH

There never was a finer day

Landscape Paintings of Wessex

with poems by Edward Thomas

front cover *May 23 (Rape Fields, Little Knoll)*
back cover *Allotments, Wessunfield*
half-title *The Lofty Sky*
frontispiece *Cart Track, Wynford Eagle*

ISBN 978 0 9544394 5 3

© Paintings by James Lynch
Poems by Edward Thomas, taken from *Edward Thomas Collected Poems*
published by Faber & Faber, 2004.
Photographs of paintings by Richard Sainsbury, Delmar Studio
Edited by Kate Lynch
Designed by Lyn Davies *lyndaviesdesign.com*
Reprographics and printing by Hampton (Bristol) Ltd

Published by Furlong Fields Publishing *furlong.fields@virgin.net*
in collaboration with:

Jonathan Cooper

Park Walk Gallery

20 Park Walk London SW10 0AQ
t +44 (0)20 7351 0410
e mail@jonathancooper.co.uk
w jonathancooper.co.uk

Contents

Wiltshire

'He rolls in the orchard: he is stained with moss
And with earth, the solitary old white horse.
Where is his father and where is his mother
Among all the brown horses? Has he a brother?
I know the swallow, the hawk, and the hern.
But there are two million things for me to learn.

'Who was the lady that rode the white horse
With rings and bells to Banbury Cross?
Was there no other lady in England beside
That a nursery rhyme could take for a ride?
The swift, the swallow, the hawk, and the hern.
There are two million things for me to learn.

'Was there a man once who straddled across
The back of the Westbury White Horse
Over there on Salisbury Plain's green wall?
Was he bound for Westbury, or had he a fall?

(continued overleaf)

Westbury White Horse details

The swift, the swallow, the hawk, and the hern.
There are two million things for me to learn.

'Out of all the white horses I know three,
At the age of six; and it seems to me
There is so much to learn, for men,
That I dare not go to bed again.
The swift, the swallow, the hawk, and the hern.
There are millions of things for me to learn.'

May 23

There never was a finer day,
And never will be while May is May, -
The third, and not the last of its kind;
But though fair and clear the two behind
Seemed pursued by tempests overpast;
And the morrow with fear that it could not last
Was spoiled. Today ere the stones were warm
Five minutes of thunderstorm
Dashed it with rain, as if to secure,
By one tear, its beauty the luck to endure.

At midday then along the lane
Old Jack Noman appeared again,
Jaunty and old, crooked and tall,
And stopped and grinned at me over the wall,
With a cowslip bunch in his button-hole
And one in his cap. Who could say if his roll
Came from flints in the road, the weather, or ale?
He was welcome as the nightingale.
Not an hour of the sun had been wasted on Jack.
'I've got my Indian complexion back'
Said he. He was tanned like a harvester,
Like his short clay pipe, like the leaf and bur
That clung to his coat from last night's bed,
Like the ploughland crumbling red.
Fairer flowers were none on the earth

(continued overleaf)

Than his cowslips wet with the dew of their birth,
Or fresher leaves than the cress in his basket.
'Where did they come from, Jack?' 'Don't ask it,
And you'll be told no lies.' 'Very well:
Then I can't buy.' 'I don't want to sell.
Take them and these flowers, too, free.
Perhaps you have something to give me?
Wait till next time. The better the day...
The Lord couldn't make a better, I say;
If he could, he never has done.'
So off went Jack with his roll-walk-run,
Leaving his cresses from Oakshott rill
And his cowslips from Wheatham hill.

'Twas the first day that the midges bit;
But though they bit me, I was glad of it:
Of the dust in my face, too, I was glad.
Spring could do nothing to make me sad.
Bluebells hid all the ruts in the copse.
The elm seeds lay in the road like hops,
That fine day, May the twenty-third,
The day Jack Noman disappeared.

May 23 (Rape Fields, Little Knoll) detail

Birds' Nests

The summer nests uncovered by autumn wind,
Some torn, others dislodged, all dark,
Everyone sees them: low or high in tree,
Or hedge, or single bush, they hang like a mark.

Since there's no need of eyes to see them with
I cannot help a little shame
That I missed most, even at eye's level, till
The leaves blew off and made the seeing no game.

'Tis a light pang. I like to see the nests
Still in their places, now first known,
At home and by far roads. Boys never found them,
Whatever jays or squirrels may have done.

And most I like the winter nest deep-hid
That leaves and berries fell into;
Once a dormouse dined there on hazel nuts;
And grass and goose-grass seeds found soil and grew.

Autumn (Wardour Park)

A Private

This ploughman dead in battle slept out of doors
Many a frosty night, and merrily
Answered staid drinkers, good bedmen, and all bores;
'At Mrs Greenland's Hawthorn Bush,' said he,
'I slept.' None knew which bush. Above the town,
Beyond 'The Drover', a hundred spot the down
In Wiltshire. And where now at last he sleeps
More sound in France - that, too, he secret keeps.

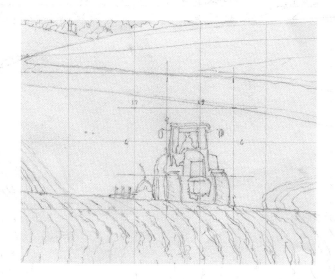

Dorset

November sky

November's days are thirty:
November's earth is dirty,
Those thirty days, from first to last;
And the prettiest things on ground are the paths
With morning and evening hobnails dinted,
With foot and wing-tip overprinted
Or separately charactered,
Of little beast and little bird.
The fields are mashed by sheep, the roads
Make the worst going, the best the woods
Where dead leaves upward and downward scatter.
Few care for the mixture of earth and water,
Twig, leaf, flint, thorn,
Straw, feather, all that men scorn,
Pounded up and sodden by flood,
Condemned as mud.

(continued overleaf)

But of all the months when earth is greener
Not one has clean skies that are cleaner.
Clean and clear and sweet and cold,
They shine above the earth so old,
While the after-tempest cloud
Sails over in silence though winds are loud,
Till the full moon in the east
Looks at the planet in the west
And earth is silent as it is black,
Yet not unhappy for its lack.
Up from the dirty earth men stare:
One imagines a refuge there
Above the mud, in the pure bright
Of the cloudless heavenly light:
Another loves earth and November more dearly
Because without them, he sees clearly,
The sky would be nothing more to his eye
Than he, in any case, is to the sky;
He loves even the mud whose dyes
Renounce all brightness to the skies.

The Gate, November details

The Lofty Sky

Today I want the sky,
The tops of the high hills,
Above the last man's house,
His hedges, and his cows,
Where, if I will, I look
Down even on sheep and rook,
And of all things that move
See buzzards only above: -
Past all trees, past furze
And thorn, where naught deters
The desire of the eye
For sky, nothing but sky.
I sicken of the woods
And all the multitudes
Of hedge-trees. They are no more
Than weeds upon this floor
Of the river of air
Leagues deep, leagues wide, where
I am like a fish that lives
In weeds and mud and gives
What's above him no thought.
I might be a tench for aught

(continued overleaf)

That I can do today
Down on the wealden clay.
Even the tench has days
When he floats up and plays
Among the lily leaves
And sees the sky, or grieves
Not if he nothing sees:
While I, I know that trees
Under that lofty sky
Are weeds, fields mud, and I
Would arise and go far
To where the lilies are.

The Lofty Sky detail

The Road (Knights Hill, West Milton)

I love roads:
The goddesses that dwell
Far along invisible
Are my favourite gods.

Roads go on
While we forget, and are
Forgotten like a star
That shoots and is gone.

On this earth 'tis sure
We men have not made
Anything that doth fade
So soon, so long endure:

The hill road wet with rain
In the sun would not gleam
Like a winding stream
If we trod it not again.

They are lonely
While we sleep, lonelier
For lack of the traveller
Who is now a dream only.

From dawn's twilight
And all the clouds like sheep
On the mountains of sleep
They wind into the night.

(continued overleaf)

The next turn may reveal
Heaven: upon the crest
The close pine clump, at rest
And black, may Hell conceal.

Often footsore, never
Yet of the road I weary,
Though long and steep and dreary
As it winds on for ever.

Helen of the roads,
The mountain ways of Wales
And the Mabinogion tales,
Is one of the true gods,

Abiding in the trees,
The threes and fours so wise,
The larger companies,
That by the roadside be,

And beneath the rafter
Else uninhabited
Excepting by the dead;
And it is her laughter

At morn and night I hear
When the thrush cock sings
Bright irrelevant things,
And when the chanticleer

Calls back to their own night
Troops that make loneliness
With their light footsteps' press,
As Helen's own are light.

Now all roads lead to France
And heavy is the tread
Of the living; but the dead
Returning lightly dance;

Whatever the road bring
To me or take from me,
They keep me company
With their pattering,

Crowding the solitude
Of the loops over the downs,
Hushing the roar of towns
And their brief multitude.

The Road, (Knights Hill, West Milton) details

Somerset

Digging (1)

Today I think
Only with scents, - scents dead leaves yield,
And bracken, and wild carrot's seed,
And the square mustard field;

Odours that rise
When the spade wounds the roots of tree,
Rose, currant, raspberry, or goutweed,
Rhubarb or celery;

The smoke's smell, too,
Flowing from where a bonfire burns
The dead, the waste, the dangerous,
And all to sweetness turns.

It is enough
To smell, to crumble the dark earth,
While the robin sings over again
Sad songs of Autumn mirth.

Allotments, Wessunfield details

Song (2)

The clouds that are so light,
Beautiful, swift and bright,
Cast shadows on field and park
Of the earth that is so dark,

And even so now, light one!
Beautiful, swift and bright one!
You let fall on a heart that was dark,
Unillumined, a deeper mark.

But clouds would have, without earth
To shadow, far less worth:
Away from your shadow on me
Your beauty less would be,

And if it still be treasured
An age hence, it shall be measured
By this small dark spot
Without which it were not.

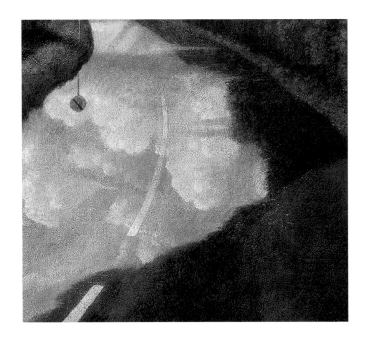

Sowing

It was a perfect day
For sowing; just
As sweet and dry was the ground
As tobacco-dust.

I tasted deep the hour
Between the far
Owl's chuckling first soft cry
And the first star.

A long stretched hour it was;
Nothing undone
Remained; the early seeds
All safely sown.

And now, hark at the rain,
Windless and light,
Half a kiss, half a tear,
Saying good-night.

Edward Thomas

by Richard Emeny, Chairman of the Edward Thomas Fellowship

Edward Thomas was born in South London on 3rd March 1878, the eldest of six sons. From an early age he enjoyed wandering over the commons of the area - Wandsworth, Wimbledon and Richmond in particular. In these places he learned about birds and plants, and he began to read the books of Richard Jefferies, whose life and writing had an enormous influence on his early life. Wiltshire became his favourite county, partly because of Jefferies and partly because the young Edward used to visit his grandmother and uncles who lived in Swindon. From there he roamed over the Marlborough Downs and North Wiltshire, covering long distances. He learned to fish, to poach, to collect birds' eggs and to follow the hunt, and he came to detest the ever growing, sprawling London.

At school his talent for writing and his imagination were recognised, and he was introduced to James Ashcroft Noble, a distinguished editor and critic. Noble encouraged the youth and placed some of his essays in magazines. He also introduced him to his daughters, one of whom, Helen, fell in love with Edward and he with her. He attended the Sixth Form at St Paul's and from there went up to Oxford, where he read history at Lincoln College. This was in the face of strong opposition from his father, a civil servant, who wanted him to follow his example.

At Oxford Thomas lived much the same life as any undergraduate, except that during this period his first book, *The Woodland Life*, was published in 1897 and Helen became pregnant. They married in secret, but when the marriage became known, both families were appalled. The situation was made worse by Edward's resolve to become a professional writer and not take regular employment. It was this decision together with the early marriage and the need to support a growing family that predicated the next fourteen years of his life. He became a hack writer: a reviewer, writer of commissioned work, a biographer and only rarely an essayist writing what he wanted rather than what he *had* to write to provide for his family. He worried ceaselessly about money and his health suffered, both physically and psychologically. Today we would probably say that he had a bipolar condition.

Amongst the books he was commissioned to write were several about the country, including *The Heart of England*, *The South Country*, *The Icknield Way* and *In Pursuit of Spring*. While he disliked writing to order, the country books at least gave him the opportunity to explore the South of England, which also became a sort of therapy against his worries and ill health. In time he came to know almost every village, footpath, small town, hill and wood in the South, especially Wiltshire, Hampshire and Kent.

Despite his problems, there were many happy and pleasant times. It was a particular satisfaction for him when he was commissioned to write a biography of his mentor, Richard Jefferies. Over the years he also became the most respected critic of his generation, writing over a million words in reviews.

The onset of war in 1914 meant the disappearance of most of his commissioned work. Fortuitously, some months before, he had met the American poet, Robert Frost, who had come to England with his family in an attempt to establish a reputation that had been denied him in America. The two men took an instant liking to each other and found that their ideas about writing poetry coincided. They were both wedded to the idea that poetry should reflect the patterns and rhythms of ordinary speech and that rhetoric had no place in its writing. Although he had experimented with verse before, it was encouragement from Frost as well as from other friends that emboldened Thomas to write verse, the war providing time that he had not

had before. This was in December 1914. He enlisted in June 1915 in the Artists Rifles, transferring to the Royal Garrison Artillery and volunteering for France in 1916. He went to the Front in late January 1917, and was killed on 9th April at the Battle of Arras by a passing shell that stopped his heart.

He wrote no poems in France, but from December 1914 until embarkation to the Front, he composed 144 poems, an extraordinary number for such a short period. They are poems often about small, insignificant events: some broken crockery seen near a ruined cottage, clay pipes, digging a vegetable patch, a copse or small stream, an old countryman. All of them tell of much more, of self investigation and the eternal questions of life and death. Many, such as 'Adlestrop' and 'Lights Out' have entered the national consciousness. It is significant that his poems have never been out of print, and perhaps even more so that many later poets from Auden to Larkin and Walcott have expressed their debt to Thomas.

It is likely that all of the landscapes in James Lynch's book would have been well known to Thomas. Both poems and pictures capture the atmosphere, depth and mystery of the country as well as representing it. Their association is a happy one.

JULY 2014.

Notes on the paintings

by James Lynch

Westbury White Horse

The horse stands under an ancient hillfort and from the top there are panoramic views across to Roundway Down, the Pewsey Vale and Devizes, my old stamping ground. The white horse is a huge landmark in Wiltshire and the old cement works used to go with it, belching out a sulphurous-smelling windsock. It's a great place to paraglide from, lovely flights down to Dorset and the coast.

Cherhill White Horse

Cherhill White Horse was first cut in 1780 under the direction of Dr. Christopher Allsop, the 'Mad Doctor'. He is supposed to have stood below the adjacent Labour-in-Vain Hill shouting instructions through a loud-hailer to the workmen. In bad weather the 19th century obelisk sometimes vanishes into the clouds over the hill. These hills and white horses and their history were the backdrop to my growing up in Wiltshire.

May 23 (Rape Fields, Little Knoll)

Litttle Knoll and Long Knoll are twin hills just south of Maiden Bradley. The B3092 runs in the pass between them. Once, some years ago, when flying from nearby Mere Down, I arrived low over here and soared on the slopes of the smaller Little Knoll, which provided just enough lift to allow me to climb away and head on down wind. The painting is the view looking east from Little Knoll towards Newmead Farm and Brimsdown Hill.

Seagulls, Brimble Lea Clump

It's a November afternoon and it's been a day of heavy showers. There's the sound of water dripping from the trees.

Autumn (Wardour Park)

The grounds of Wardour Castle. In May 1643 the sound of cannons would have filled the air. Lady Blanche Arundell and

her garrison of twenty-five soldiers and a few servants were under siege by the Parliamentarians.

The Ploughman, White Sheet Hill

Mere Down, looking North. Next to Kingston Deverill Church there are three old sarcens which once stood on the hill above. The story goes that Alfred mustered an army there before his battle at Edington. Are the defeated Vikings remembered in Danes Bottom, a stone's throw from the church? It's early April, windy, a day of showers passing through and there's a rumbling from the distant guns on Salisbury Plain.

Rainbow's End

A day of big clouds, hail, heavy showers and sunny intervals. I was hoping to catch the light on the landscape from Little Knoll and all the way down the A303 the bad weather was running in front of me. I climbed the hill in the dry but then

it went dark and there was a massive downpour. For a quarter of an hour I crouched in the woods on the lea side of the hill and waited for the squall to pass through. When it cleared I climbed back up to the top, and there was the rainbow.

The Gate, November

These cirrus clouds are miles up. There's a cold light and it's in the water in the tractor ruts – the mud's reflecting the light from thousands of feet up. This painting was inspired by Edward Thomas' poem 'November Sky'.

The Lofty Sky

Under the sea-breeze convergence clouds, standing on Bulbarrow Hill, looking south towards Nettlecombe Tout – a meeting place of five ancient trackways, and about as remote a spot as you can find in Dorset. It gets a mention in Thomas Hardy's 'Tess of the d'Urbevilles':

"If Tess were made rich by marrying a gentleman, would she have money enough to buy a spy-glass so large that it would draw the stars as near to her as Nettlecombe Tout?"

The Road (Knights Hill, West Milton)

For some years I've been drawn to the Dorset landscape, around Powerstock and West Milton – sunken lanes, ancient forests and a glimpse of the sea in the dips between the hills. The late Kenneth Allsop lived here when he wrote 'In the Country', an evocative collection of anecdotes and observations about the place.

Ruscombe Lane (Powerstock)

Approaching Powerstock from the north, down the winding Ruscombe Lane, there are fine views to the south – Chilcombe and Shipton Hills on the horizon, Eggardon Hill to the left, out of sight. There's a particular quality of light here in the autumn and winter time at the end of a bright day, at around half past three when the sun is low.

Stout Hill (High Ham)

The journey home. I walk, jog and cycle this lane many times a week, our house just out of sight at the top of the hill. This is an old route from the low wet moor to the ridge above. Further up, the road has been worn down, cut deep over time by people, animals and the wheels of carts. It is February, it's been raining and in the mud there's the memory of John's tractor.

Allotments, Wessunfield

As a war artist Eric Ravilious was briefly stationed here at RAF Westonzoyland on the Somerset Levels. These allotments have been created by the community from part of the old airfield. I'm drawn to these old Second World War airfields with their huge skies and noisy history. They are often bleak

and silent places – but here there is the ordered paraphernalia of devoted gardeners and it's a place of sanctuary.

Cumulonimbus over Glastonbury Tor

This is a cumulonimbus cloud, it's the big one. This one's probably 20,000 feet already. It's pushed through the altostratus layers and it's moving upwards and expanding. Then, when it runs out of steam, it will collapse and spread into the classic anvil. It's a menacing force – in paragliding circles this is the one to avoid, it can pull you in, suck you up and spit you out, it's the stuff of hyperthermia, frostbite and canopy collapse.

The Clouds that are so Light (Othery from Turn Hill)

A view from Turn Hill, one of the best viewpoints in Somerset – on the edge of the village where I live. It looks out over Beer Wood and across North Moor to Little England and Othery. Last winter, the moor below was flooded for three months

and the main road across it was submerged until they imported gigantic pumps from the Netherlands to pump it dry.

The Muchelney Road

The road flooded, July 2012. On this day we walked as far as we could until the bow wave of a passing landrover filled our boots. Then in the following two winters there were more floods and Muchelney became an island in an inland sea. Prince Charles was ferried in on a pontoon decked with garlands. Now they are dredging the rivers and building bunds to hold back future floods.

It was a Perfect Day

From my studio on a ridge above the Somerset Levels, I look north across King's Sedgemoor. Ted's house and garden is below, hidden by trees. I often walk or cycle down the hill, along the lane and past his greenhouse. Today the cumulonimbus cloud on the horizon is losing its energy and the last of the day's showers has moved down wind. It's been a perfect day for sowing.

Ted's Greenhouse, Winter

A cold winter's afternoon. A walk down along Cooke's Lane and past Ted's greenhouse and vegetable garden, and back round by Wishell Farm with its herd of dairy cows warm in the barn.

65

Egg tempera

by James Lynch

Egg tempera was widely used by medieval and Renaissance painters until it was superseded by oil paint. I have been using the medium for over twenty years and originally took my instructions from the Quattrocento manual written by Cennino Cennini.

I make my own gesso ground from rabbit skin glue and whiting according to a traditional recipe, painting several layers of the creamy paste onto a wood panel as the support for the painting. I mix my own paint from the raw ground pigments, egg yolk and water and adjust the watery paint over the course

of the painting, moving from a 'leaner' mix with less yolk in the water in the early stages of the painting, to a 'fatter' mix with a little more yolk in the later stages. I use eggs from hens I keep below my studio.

Egg tempera is applied in thin layers and each painting is the result of scores of glazes, building up the brilliant richness of colour slowly. The paint glazes are translucent and allow light to bounce back from the underlying white gesso ground, and egg tempera paintings have a unique glow.

Egg tempera is very light-fast and does not darken and yellow over time as oil paintings do. Although egg tempera fell out of favour in the late Renaissance, it was rediscovered by later artists such as William Blake and the Pre-Raphaelites. It's nice to know I am continuing an ancient painting tradition.

Curriculum Vitæ

Born 1956, grew up in Devizes, Wiltshire.
Took up paragliding in 2002. Lives on the Somerset Levels.

Exhibitions

2014
'There never was a Finer Day'
Jonathan Cooper, Park Walk Gallery, London
w jonathancooper.co.uk

2011
'The Inhabited Landscape'
Jonathan Cooper, Park Walk Gallery, London

2006
Maas Gallery, London

2004
Black Swan, Frome, Somerset

2001, 2003
Maas Gallery

2000
Alpha House Gallery, Sherborne, Dorset

1999
Maas Gallery

1998
Retrospective, Mompesson House, Salisbury, Wiltshire
(National Trust Foundation for Art)

1991, 93, 95, 97
Maas Gallery

1988
Odette Gilbert, London

1984, 85, 86
Nevill Gallery, Bath

1983
Linfield Galleries, Bradford-on-Avon

Also represented in the following group shows:
Christie's and Agnews, London; Galerie Michael, Beverley Hills, USA; National Trust Foundation for Art Exhibitions; Royal Academy Summer Exhibitions, and others.

Publications

There Never Was a Finer Day, pub. Furlong Fields Publishing in collaboration with Jonathan Cooper, Park Walk Gallery 2014; *Skylines*, pub. Furlong Fields Publishing 2006; Illustrations for *The Wind in the Willows* by Kenneth Grahame, pub. Folio Society 1995.

Collections

Chatsworth House; C. Hoare & Co.; National Trust Foundation for Art (Chartwell, Kent; Kingston Lacy, Dorset; Wimpole Hall, Cambridgeshire); Wessex Collection, Longleat House; and other private collections

w *james-lynch.co.uk*

Index of paintings

The Wessex Ridgway (Knoyle Corner)

Acknowledgements

I am grateful to the executors of the Edward Thomas
Estate and to Richard Emeny, Chairman of the Edward
Thomas Fellowship. Thanks to my wife, Kate, for
editing the book and Jonathan Cooper and Alice
Phillimore, Park Walk Gallery, for their support.

James Lynch

from Interval

Gone the wild day.
A wilder night
Coming makes way
For brief twilight.

Ted's Greenhouse, Winter